CAREERS MAKING A DIFFERENCE

# HELPING ANIMALS

# CAREERS MAKING A DIFFERENCE

HELPING ANIMALS

HELPING CHILDREN

HELPING SENIORS

HELPING THOSE IN POVERTY

HELPING THOSE WITH ADDICTIONS

HELPING THOSE WITH DISABILITIES

HELPING THOSE WITH MENTAL ILLNESSES

HELPING TO PROTECT THE ENVIRONMENT

HELPING VICTIMS

CAREERS MAKING A DIFFERENCE

# HELPING ANIMALS

AMANDA TURNER

MASON CREST

PHILADELPHIA
MIAMI

# MASON CREST

450 Parkway Drive, Suite D, Broomall, Pennsylvania 19008
(866) MCP-BOOK (toll-free) • www.masoncrest.com

Printed in the United States of America

First printing
9 8 7 6 5 4 3 2 1

ISBN (hardback) 978-1-4222-4254-4
ISBN (series) 978-1-4222-4253-7
ISBN (ebook) 978-1-4222-7540-5

Cataloging-in-Publication Data on file with the Library of Congress

Developed and produced by National Highlights Inc.
Editor: Susan Uttendorfsky
Interior and cover design: Torque Advertising + Design
Production: Michelle Luke

## QR CODES AND LINKS TO THIRD-PARTY CONTENT

# TABLE OF CONTENTS

# KEY ICONS TO LOOK FOR

**Words to Understand:** These words with their easy-to-understand definitions will increase the reader's understanding of the text while building vocabulary skills.

**Sidebars:** This boxed material within the main text allows readers to build knowledge, gain insights, explore possibilities, and broaden their perspectives by weaving together additional information to provide realistic and holistic perspectives.

**Educational Videos:** Readers can view videos by scanning our QR codes, providing them with additional educational content to supplement the text. Examples include news coverage, moments in history, speeches, iconic sports moments, and much more!

**Text-Dependent Questions:** These questions send the reader back to the text for more careful attention to the evidence presented there.

**Research Projects:** Readers are pointed toward areas of further inquiry connected to each chapter. Suggestions are provided for projects that encourage deeper research and analysis.

**Series Glossary of Key Terms:** This back-of-the-book glossary contains terminology used throughout this series. Words found here increase the reader's ability to read and comprehend higher-level books and articles in this field.

# AWARENESS OF THE CAUSE

For centuries, animals have been by our sides as friends, workers, hunters, and even our food. Over time, we have domesticated some of them to suit our needs, while others remain wild. Sadly, due to our activities, many species are now endangered. Fortunately, though, our close association with the animal world has now prompted us to take responsibility for animals to ensure their welfare and protection. Today, there is a growing acceptance that all animals should be treated humanely and fairly.

*"For as long as men massacre animals, they will kill each other."*
– Pythagoras

*"The love for all living creatures is the most noble attribute of man."*
– Charles Darwin

*"It is just like a man's vanity and impertinence to call an animal dumb."*
– Mark Twain

*"The greatness of a nation and its moral progress can be judged by the way animals are treated."*
K. Gandhi

# CHAPTER 1

# Is a Career Helping Animals for You?

*Most people have a worthy cause that they believe in. You can even work in this field yourself by following a career and making a difference to society.*

- Start out as a volunteer.
- Seek out a personal connection in the field.
- Develop an inspirational mission statement for yourself.
- Find out about the education, training, and qualifications required for your chosen career.
- Study job specifications of interest.
- Discuss your goals with your loved ones.
- Approach school counselors, charities, and organizations to obtain advice.

# RIGHTS OF ANIMALS

A recent study found that 32 percent of Americans agree that animals should have the same rights as people.

## ANIMALS IN AGRICULTURE AND INDUSTRY

According to the U.S. Department of Agriculture, the total number of land animals slaughtered for food in the United States has ranged between 8.9 and 9.5 billion since 2000.

- The United States is a major producer of leather. It is one of the world's largest producer of bovine hide and exports all over the world.

- Americans trap and kill more wild animals for fur than any other country (up to 7 million annually).

## PET OWNERSHIP

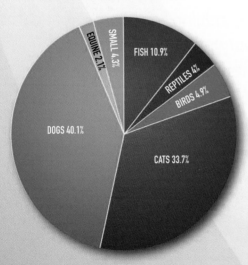

FISH 10.9%
SMALL 4.3%
EQUINE 2.1%
REPTILES 4%
BIRDS 4.9%
DOGS 40.1%
CATS 33.7%

SOURCE: Lend a Helping Paw.

## CATS AND DOGS

- It's estimated that 78 million dogs and 85.8 million cats are owned in the United States. Approximately 40.1 percent of all households in the United States have a dog, and 33.7 percent have a cat.

- APPA (American Pet Products Association) reports that 34 percent of dogs are purchased from breeders, while 23 percent of dogs and 31 percent of cats are obtained from an animal shelter or humane society.

## UNWANTED ANIMALS

The ASPCA's (Association for the Prevention of Cruelty to Animals) National Rehoming Survey, states that pet problems are the most common reason that owners rehome their pet.

- There are approximately 200,000 unwanted horses annually in the United States. Many are shipped to slaughter, enter rescue facilities, or are held on federal lands.

- More than 1 million animals die each day on roads in the United States. Road mortality is the leading cause of vertebrate deaths in the United States.

### 10 ANIMAL CHARITIES

1. ASPCA
2. Friends of Animals
3. PetSmart Charities
4. Performing Animal Welfare Society (PAWS)
5. D.E.L.T.A. Rescue
6. American Humane
7. Best Friends Animal Society
8. Wildlife Conservation Society
9. Humane Farming Association
10. The Marine Mammal Center

## AMERICA'S MOST ENDANGERED SPECIES

Examples include: the red wolf, pygmy racoon, H.J. Franklin's bumblebee, the California condor, the Vancouver marmot, the pygmy raccoon, the Oahu tree snail, Kemp's ridley turtle, the panther, the Columbia basin pygmy rabbit, the Eskimo curlew, the Ramsey Canyon leopard frog, the dusky gopher frog, the smalltooth sawfish, the Mitchell's satyr butterfly, the bog turtle, the gray fox.

## DID YOU KNOW?

- Animal charities receive less money than charities that help humans.

- Each year, animal charities carry out vital work in helping to work toward improving animal welfare through raising awareness of animal cruelty and directly providing care to animals in need.

- Helping animals is good for your emotional, physical, and mental health.

# AWARENESS OF THE CAUSE

**ORGANIZATIONS THAT HELP ANIMALS**

6 — Animal Shelters
1 — Police
2 — Conservation Groups
3 — Veterinarian Practices
4 — Helplines
5 — ASPCA

## HOW CAN YOU HELP AN ANIMAL IN NEED?

- Seek veterinary advice
- If a crime has been committed, report it to the police
- Take the animal to safety
- Seek professional help
- Seek practical help
- Make a financial donation
- Donate your time
- Educate others

# THE BENEFITS OF HELPING OTHERS

## A SENSE OF PURPOSE

*Helping animals provides a sense of purpose to an individual. People who volunteer for a cause feel that their life is worthwhile and satisfying. This ultimately leads to improved physical and emotional health.*

## EMOTIONAL HEALTH

*Studies have also shown that the act of charity results in emotional well-being. The person who gives to charity feels improved self-esteem. This gives a feeling of satisfaction to the individual. In a way, giving to others allows the individual to create a "kindness bank account." The more kind acts are filled in the account the better the emotional state of the person.*

## A HEALTHY HEART

*A recent study found that there is a significant correlation between helping animals and the heart's health. It was found that people who volunteer are about 40 percent less likely to develop high blood pressure as compared to those who do not volunteer.*

## HELPING OTHERS MAKES YOU HAPPY

*According to research, people who engage in acts of kindness and giving are happier in general as compared to others. Acts of kindness carried out regularly or even once a week can lead to greater happiness and joy in life.*

## REDUCE STRESS

*The act of helping can also help reduce stress. Research shows that people who help have lower cortisol levels. The presence of this hormone in the body causes it to create feelings of anxiety and panic, which can lead to higher blood pressure levels. People who do less for others have a higher level of the stress hormone in their body.*

## ANIMAL WELFARE ACT

Prior to the passing of the Animal Welfare Act, or AWA, there were no federal laws regulating the treatment of animals in scientific research labs, and many experiments were performed on animals that would be considered cruel and inhumane by today's standards. Many of the scientists conducting research said that the testing was necessary to determine the safety of products for humans (such as cosmetics, foods, and medicines), but the ways that the experiments were conducted were often unnecessarily brutal and painful for the animals. Passed in 1966, the AWA is the only federal law in the United States that regulates animal treatment in the area of research.

When the AWA was originally created, many research facilities were stealing pets and using them for laboratory tests. Pet owners began to demand a law that would hold people responsible for committing pet theft. Originally, the law specified only how animals could be obtained and how they were required to be cared for at the lab facility—there was no regulation on the experiments that researchers could and could not perform on animals.

While the law was originally created to protect laboratory only research animals, today it also protects the rights of animals during exhibitions, sale, and transport. It specifies the standards of care that must be upheld for animals in research labs and other settings, including food, exercise, and the types of experiments that may be performed.

There are other animal welfare regulations that are specific for certain species and in certain situations, but those laws refer to the AWA as the gold standard for how animals are to be treated. This rule has been expanded over time to meet the needs of animals due to lobbyists fighting for animal rights. It has been revised and amended many times, with the most recent amendments added in 2013.

Today, the law covers many facets of animal well-being, including regulations and restrictions on fighting, protection for domestic pets, regulations for treatment of farm animals, and restrictions on the experiments that can be performed on lab animals.

**conservation:** the caretaking and supervision of natural areas (lakes, oceans, forests) and the animals and plants that they contain with the goal of protecting these resources through careful management

**endangered species:** a specific type of plant or animal that is likely to become extinct in the near future

**threatened:** the stage in species conservation that comes before "endangered"; species may become endangered if corrective action is not taken

**welfare:** the overall well-being of a living organism

# CHAPTER 2

# Why Work with Animals?

## DECIDING TO WORK WITH ANIMALS

Love taking care of your pets? Interested in learning more about becoming a dog trainer? Curious about what it's like to work for an animal rescue center? If you're considering devoting your career to helping animals, you may be overwhelmed at all the different career path options, from charity work to business to direct care. There's a lot to consider:

- Do you want to work directly with the animals?
- Do you want to fight for stricter government laws on how animals should be treated?
- Do you want to go through years of schooling to become a veterinarian?
- Are you looking for a job you can begin immediately after high school or college graduation?

# WHY I WANT TO HELP HORSES

I have been enchanted with horses for as long as I can remember. I was attracted rather than intimidated by their great size and as a tiny child wanted nothing more than to be with them, to smell their sweet breath, to hear their neighs and the sound of their hooves resonating on the ground. Many would think that loving horses is all about riding them, but to me it was the entire relationship, built up over the years, that is the most rewarding part.

When I first joined the local riding school, I knew that learning to ride horses was not going to be enough or me, so I became involved with their mucking out, grooming, and other duties around the stable yard.

I completed my education a year ago and now work at an animal shelter that takes in unwanted equines. I find my work very rewarding. It gives me great satisfaction to see the animals in my care regain their health and learn to trust again.—Robert Norris.

No matter which path you choose, you will be doing something amazing by helping creatures who cannot help themselves. Let's discuss some different avenues that you can take to help make the world a better and safer place for animals.

## ANIMAL SHELTER WORKER

Animal shelters house animals that have been found as strays or turned over by owners who are no longer able to care for them. When a pregnant animal is brought to a shelter, the shelter takes on the care of the baby animals as well. Often, animals that have been turned over to shelters are scared and in need of health care. Along with providing a place for creatures that do not have homes, shelters typically also provide free or low-cost health care to animal owners who have a financial need.

It takes a compassionate, caring animal lover to fulfill the role of an animal shelter worker. Employees at shelters can be responsible for a variety

*If you choose a career working with animals, it stands to reason that you should be an ardent animal lover.*

of different tasks. A new animal shelter worker may be asked to work at the front desk, answer the phone, clean out crates and litter boxes, feed animals, and/or and administer medication to sick animals. Shelters often can't afford to hire many paid staff members and depend on volunteers to keep the shelter running.

Paid employees may be responsible for volunteer outreach, volunteer scheduling, and training volunteers, as well as caring for animals, keeping track of how many spaces the shelter has for animals in need, and facilitating adoptions. After training, shelter employees may be able to take on basic medical care, including surgical aftercare. Many veterinarians work at shelters and depend

*Animal shelter workers have a whole range of tasks to complete during their shifts. In this case, an orphaned lamb requires regular bottle-feeding.*

on paid trained employees to assist them in performing medical procedures, such as spaying and/or neutering pets before they are adopted. Paid employees are also responsible for screening potential adopters and ensuring that they are a good match for the pet they have selected.

As an animal shelter worker, you may also be responsible for following up with people who have adopted animals, ensuring that the animal is settling in well at their new home.

*Animal shelter workers are usually employed in kennels, animal rescue centers, or sanctuaries. They can also work in charity-run animal hospitals or adoption centers.*

To increase the number of adoptions, shelters frequently hold special events at grocery stores, pet food stores, and community events. Shelter staff members bring animals to meet and greet the general public, and these events can be wonderful chances for animal shelter workers to show off the animals available for adoption.

You may be responsible for organizing these events, setting up a tent or booth, transporting animals to the event, and helping potential adopters fill out the required paperwork.

Working in a shelter can be difficult emotionally, but it can also be very rewarding. It is hard to go home without taking the ones you have come to love with you, but no one can take them all home. It's a balancing act to love and care for the creatures at the shelter and be able to leave your job after your shift without experiencing a lot of sadness.

## WORKING WITH RESCUED HORSES, MULES, AND DONKEYS

Equine rescue is a growing field, as there are over 177,000 unwanted horses in the United States each year. That number does not include the thousands of unwanted donkeys and mules that are also in need of rescue. Unfortunately, there are many reasons why a horse owner no longer wants their horse (or mule or donkey). Sometimes these animals have injured riders, or are likely to injure riders, and the owner no longer feels that they are able to control the animal.

*Thousands of horses and other equines become unwanted every year; therefore, equine rescue centers play a vital role in providing care for these abandoned animals. Working at one of these centers can be both rewarding and worthwhile.*

Some of them no longer perform at the level that was expected—this is especially true of racehorses. It's sad, but many horse owners see their animal as a business, a tool to win prize money rather than a living being that deserves care regardless of their athletic performance. Other than horse racing, equines can be wonderful furry members for families, but owners are often overwhelmed by the time and money required to care for these large pets. On average, it costs nearly $2,500 each year to care for a healthy horse. In a recent survey, owners who surrendered their equine stated that a change in their situation—such as becoming unemployed and no longer having the financial means to care of their horse—was the number-one reason for giving up their animal. When horses are abandoned, they are often sent to slaughterhouses in Canada and Mexico (as horse slaughter is banned in the United States) and the meat is then sent to other countries for human consumption.

*While the majority of us associate equine rescue centers with horses, donkeys and mules can also be abandoned. Hopefully, this young donkey will be rehomed in the future.*

Unfortunately, horses are not as simple to rehome as dogs and cats. Even though many people like the idea of having a horse, few have the knowledge, resources, and space necessary to ensure a happy life for an equine. When owners are unable to or neglect to care for their horses, equine rescue has to step in. There are not nearly enough equine rescue organizations in the United States to care for the number of unwanted animals that currently exist.

Working for an equine rescue shelter can involve a number of tasks, such as locating and arranging transportation for animals in need, working to help provide owners with financial assistance for horse health care, coordinating health care with veterinarians, and providing hands-on horse care. As more media attention is directed to equine rescue, more funds are becoming available for these organizations through private donors. The number of equine rescue organizations in the United States will probably continue to grow over time.

## CHARITY FUNDRAISER FOR ANIMAL WELFARE

If you love event planning and animals, becoming a charity fundraiser for animal welfare organizations may be the right path for you. Most animal shelters are underfunded and in dire need of financial support. By becoming a charity fundraiser, you have the ability to give shelters the money that they need to provide for the animals in their care.

Charity fundraisers can take on a variety of roles, from connecting animal welfare organizations with fundraising opportunities to organizing/hosting large benefit events. Some charity fundraisers work for companies that put together all sorts of different fundraisers for different

*There are many ways of raising money for animal welfare. Charities are always looking for volunteers to help them with their cause.*

organizations. Other charity fundraisers work with one specific organization, such as the ASPCA, coordinating their fundraising efforts with others to benefit the same organization. Many charity benefits are essentially huge parties with a big price tag on each ticket, with the proceeds going to an animal welfare organization.

As a fundraiser, your job could entail serious event planning. These galas are no small feat—it takes someone with impeccable organizational skills and a flair for design to put together a fantastic fundraising event. In addition to parties, charity fundraisers often organize large auctions with expensive or one-of-a-kind items that attendees bid on, with proceeds going to the charity organization. You may be in charge of contacting area businesses, past donors, and local celebrities for big-ticket items (such as jewelry, vacations, cruises, memorabilia) and asking them to donate to the auction. You might need to provide donors with tax information and write thank-you notes after the auction. You'll also likely work with ticketing, seating charts, catering, and entertainment. If you're someone who enjoys planning parties and interacting with people, charity fundraising could be a great option for you!

## CHARITY WORKER

There are a vast number of animal charities in the United States, and all of them have different roles that need to be filled. If you are interested in working for an animal charity, you'll probably be able to find an

*The Best Friends Animal Society hosts an annual Strut Your Mutt walk and fundraiser in New York City. At this event, money is raised for rescue groups, shelters, and animal welfare in general.*

*There are plenty of ways of raising money for a chosen charity. This office team has set up donation boxes for unwanted clothing. The clothing can be sold to raise funds.*

organization that works to protect the welfare of your favorite animal(s). From dogs and cats to reptiles, there are people working to raise money to protect the rights of different groups of animals worldwide.

The great thing about working for an animal charity organization is that there are typically a variety of employment opportunities, including human resources, accounting, volunteer management, communications, technology, outreach, and writing educational literature. These organizations run like any other business, plus they are passionate about helping animals. Animal charity work is a great way to combine your academic or business passion with your love for animals. Many times, animal charities also

*As well as providing practical help in the process of fundraising, there is also a great need for administrative staff who can keep accounts and records relating to the fundraising activity.*

provide the opportunity to work directly with the animals as a direct-care worker or as a veterinarian. It's also possible to be a volunteer for animal charities, especially if you work in a high-demand field such as animal medical care. Animal charities will frequently allow you to donate your professional services to them as a charitable donation.

## CONSERVATION WORKER

As a **conservation** worker, you'll be contributing to the important cause of protecting **endangered species** from extinction. Much like animal welfare organizations, conservation societies are often vast nonprofit organizations that have many different employment and volunteer opportunities. Scientists and biologists are often employed by conservation organizations. These

*Many of today's zoos work hard to conserve species that are endangered in the wild. They employ scientists and zoologists as well as animal carers.*

professionals study endangered and **threatened** species and learn what humans can do to protect them. Conservation organizations also employ human resources experts, accountants, advertising professionals, and educators.

Education is a large goal of conservation organizations. Conservation workers often give presentations in museums and schools about animals and the environment, helping students to understand how their choices affect the world around them. If you're passionate about conservation, there are many different ways that you can help at a conservation organization.

## ANIMAL NURSE

Just like human patients, animals sometimes need direct medical care, especially after undergoing a medical procedure such as a surgery. Animal nurses are just the people for the job.

Veterinary offices, animal rescue centers, and animal shelters often employ nurses. Some nurses treat a variety of animals, while others specialize in certain areas, such as equine care.

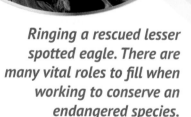

*Ringing a rescued lesser spotted eagle. There are many vital roles to fill when working to conserve an endangered species.*

*An animal nurse is an essential part of a veterinary medical team. Animal nurses perform routine medical procedures on a daily basis along with record-keeping and communicating with the patients' owners.*

*Just like regular nurses, animal nurses are highly skilled. They are trained to be knowledgeable about a variety of species.*

An animal nurse is an important part of any veterinary medical team, and they work closely with surgeons and veterinarians, providing round-the-clock care, including administering intravenous medication, caring for surgical wounds, and monitoring animals with a critical need for constant care. Just like nurses in human hospitals, animal nurses often work long hours so they can spend a lot of time with specific animals during each shift. Along with providing direct care to animals, animal nurses also perform routine medical procedures, collect samples for the lab, and maintain medical records. Some animal nurses are even able to provide checkups in veterinary offices.

Many animal nurses are also trained in emergency medicine and are able to perform lifesaving procedures on animals in need. If you are considering becoming a veterinarian, working as an animal nurse before attending veterinary school will give you some insight into whether the field of animal medical treatment is a good fit for your interests.

# FOSTER CARE WORKER

Many shelters do not have enough resources or space to take care of all the animals in need in their area. This is where animal foster care comes in! This program matches foster animals with "parents" who can take in animals in need of a home for a short period of time until a permanent home can be found. Sometimes foster parents work to connect the animal with potential adopters. They may do this through community organizations or through social media.

Other times, finding potential adopters is the job of the animal foster care worker. Foster care workers may provide foster parents with the items they need to take care of their animals, such as crates, bedding, food, and flea and tick treatment. Often these items are donated to animal shelters, and animal foster care workers make sure these supplies get into the homes of the foster parents who need them. Other times, the foster parent is provided with a small amount of money in order to help them purchase these items.

*Sometimes animal shelters get very crowded. During these times, foster "parents" take in animals for limited periods.*

Fostering is frequently used when a dog or cat has a litter of babies, allowing the mother to take care of the babies for a longer period of time than if they were in a shelter. Foster parents take care of the animals as if they were their own, training then when appropriate, working on housebreaking, and providing them with love and care. Animal foster care workers have many important tasks: they may be in charge of finding volunteer foster parents, screening parents to make sure they are suitable to foster, conducting welfare checks on the animals in foster care, and facilitating the adoption process when it's time for an animal to come out of foster care. Animal foster care workers may also be responsible for finding low-cost medical care for animals to help offset the costs for foster parents. Animal foster work can be emotionally taxing but incredibly rewarding.

## ANIMAL RESCUE

The thousands of animals that are abused and neglected each year have a special group of heroes—animal rescue workers. Rescue workers are often involved in the direct care of neglected, injured, and abused animals. This can involve removing frightened and sick animals from abusive or neglectful situations, such as pets that are left outside without shelter from excessive cold or heat, are not provided with enough food, or who have medical conditions that are not being treated.

Rescue organizations often work in tandem with law enforcement to legally remove animals from harmful situations. Sometimes law

*Animal rescue workers are involved in the direct care of neglected, injured, and abused animals.*

*Unfortunately, some domestic pets are rescued from terrible conditions. Sometimes, law enforcement gets involved.*

enforcement officers will call animal rescues when they see an animal in need in hopes that the rescue can take in the animal and help them find a loving forever home.

Animal rescues often have their own facilities to house and treat animals, but sometimes rescues simply work to connect animals in need with other shelters and/or foster homes. Animal rescue centers typically employ veterinarians and animal nurses that specialize in lifesaving animal care, as the majority of the animals that come into these facilities are in dire need of medical attention. Many animals arrive at an extremely low weight, and it's important that skilled, experienced veterinarians handle the process of getting these animals back up to a healthy weight. An unknowing benefactor who feeds them too much too quickly might unintentionally trigger additional health problems, or even the animal's death. Rescue facilities also employ behavior specialists, as many rescued animals need special training to overcome the abuse that they may have experienced.

Animal rescue workers have shifts that are different from that of a typical shelter, as the rescue centers are often called at all hours of the day and night to help animals in need. Often it's key that rescue workers act quickly, as minutes may make the difference between life and death for a suffering animal.

Due to the unique situations that many animals in rescue have lived through and overcome, most animal rescue organizations employ adoption counselors. These professionals work with potential adopters to make sure that they understand the needs of their potential new pet. Adoption counselors need to be experts on the animals that they work with so that they are able to explain any medical and psychological conditions in detail.

The job of an adoption counselor does not stop after the rescue animal is adopted. Just like shelter workers, adoption counselors often need to follow up with adopters to find out how the pet is adjusting to their new life, and see if the adopter is in need of any additional resources to care for their new family member.

*A typical workday for a veterinarian is largely dependent on their specialty. Veterinarians who treat equines often travel some distances between each patient.*

# VETERINARIAN

While most veterinary offices treat domestic pets such as dogs and cats, there are a wide variety of specialty areas that veterinarians can choose from. Specialized veterinarians exist for every category of animal, from birds to marine animals to horses.

A typical workday for a veterinarian is largely dependent on their specialty. A vet who specializes in dogs may work a typical 9–5 job in an office, while a vet who specializes in marine animals may work very different hours treating beached ocean animals or working nights at an aquarium. Vets are also needed on large farms or in zoos. Depending on the type of animal they work with, vets may simply work on call, meaning they respond whenever they get a call requesting care for a sick animal.

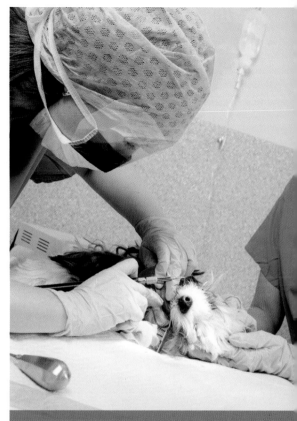

*This veterinarian is performing a dental procedure on a Yorkshire terrier.*

Veterinarians provide all types of medical care to animals, including surgery. They also have the emotional and difficult job of working with pet owners to decide when the time is right to euthanize (end the life of) an animal due to a progressive disease or a devastating injury.

Out of all the different options for careers that work with animals, being a veterinarian requires the most extensive schooling. Unlike a human doctor—who only has to learn about people—vets have to learn how to care for a lot of animals that may be very different from each other. Veterinarians typically make more money than other animal care professions, but they usually also need to pay back school loans for many years after they finish graduate school. While vets have a difficult job, there is nothing like ending the day knowing that you've saved an animal's life!

# ZOOLOGIST

To a visitor, a zoo is simply a place to look at exciting animals (and maybe catch an animal education presentation), but there is a lot that goes on behind the scenes! Zoologists (also known as animal biologists) are scientists who study the animal kingdom. Some don't just study animals but work in zoos, providing medical care. This does not only mean helping animals when they get hurt or sick.

Zoologists are experts in what animals need to eat to thrive. They know how much exercise animals need, how much they need to socialize with others, and how much space they need to feel comfortable. Many zoologists work with endangered species, trying to increase their populations so they can be removed from the endangered list.

While zoologists do a lot of behind-the-scenes work, many also enjoy giving presentations to people visiting the zoo to help them learn more about their favorite animals. Some zoologists are experts in animal behavior and help decide which animals can be together in the same exhibit.

Zoologists may also work in the wild, treating animals that have been injured. This type of work is especially important for animal species that are experiencing a decline in the number of individual animals that are alive. The hard work of zoologists can save entire populations from becoming extinct. They may be able to treat the animal and release it back into the wild, or they may need to bring the animal into captivity, either temporarily or permanently, in order to allow the animal to live out its life.

*This zoologist is studying mongooses and their behavior at the Moscow Zoo.*

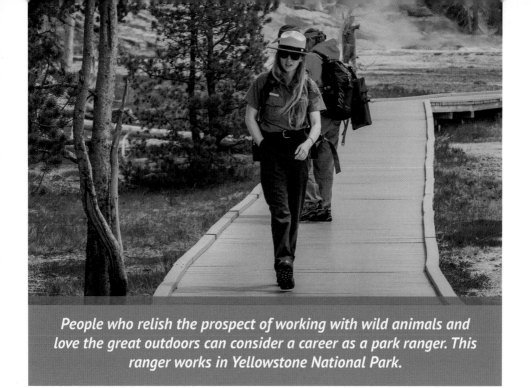

*People who relish the prospect of working with wild animals and love the great outdoors can consider a career as a park ranger. This ranger works in Yellowstone National Park.*

Zoologists always keep the best interests of the animals at heart, not what is easiest. It's important to note that this can be a hazardous profession—working with wild animals is exciting, but they can be unpredictable, large, or dangerous, and used to defending themselves physically. While the zoologist only wants to help, the animals don't know that.

## NATIONAL PARK RANGER

If you enjoy spending time in the great outdoors, becoming a national parks ranger might be a good idea for you. Rangers are responsible for protecting national parks, and this includes being responsible for the animals within the park. Park rangers need to keep an eye on the wildlife of the park and make sure that animals are healthy and safe. This means protecting animals from illegal hunters, pollutants, and other threats, as well as educating campers and hikers on how to enjoy wildlife without getting hurt and without hurting the animals.

Park rangers rarely work one-on-one with animals, as they are focused on keeping animals safe in their natural habitat, unbothered by people. While being a national park ranger has a lot of upsides, it can be hard if you prefer spending a lot of time around people. Most park rangers patrol the park grounds by themselves.

# WHAT ARE THE HOURS LIKE?

It's important to consider the hours for the specific job you're interested in working toward when you pursue a career in animal welfare. Some professions, such as emergency veterinarians and animal rescuers, work around the clock and often have shifts late at night. Other careers, such as a veterinarian in a non-emergency office or a charity fundraiser, are likely to have more typical working hours. If you're interested in helping animals, there is a career path that fits your desired schedule—you just have to find it!

# THINKING ABOUT BECOMING A VETERINARIAN

*Learn how to achieve a career in veterinary science*

If yes you should consider becoming a veterinarian

# TEXT-DEPENDENT QUESTIONS

1. Why does an animal rescue organization need adoption counselors?

2. What is a foster parent for animals?

3. What is one of the daily tasks of a national parks ranger?

# RESEARCH PROJECT

Interview someone who is employed in one of the fields listed in this chapter. Find out how they chose to go into that field, what they like about their job, what they wish they could change about their job, and what type of education they needed to begin their career.

# Milestone Moment

## ENDANGERED SPECIES ACT

Passed in 1973, the Endangered Species Act (ESA) provided a framework for protecting endangered species (both plants and animals) and their environments. Prior to the passage of the ESA, there were no laws to keep endangered animals and plants safe. Corporations often built on land that was home to endangered animals, causing their populations to dwindle. Many factories disposed of their waste in unsafe ways that harmed the environment and the drinking water that animals were dependent on for their survival. The ESA put a stop to this type of destruction.

Through the ESA, the federal government provides individual state governments with financial resources to create and implement conservation programs that help to protect the endangered species in that particular state. The ESA has allowed many animals—including the California condor, the grizzly bear, and the black-footed ferret—to be brought back from near-extinction. The ESA requires many different entities, including state, local, and federal governments, nonprofit organizations, and private organizations, to work together to decide the best way to serve and protect endangered species.

The ESA's main focus is on recovering species that are close to extinction and preventing species from getting to that point in the first place. The ESA's initiatives are based in science and research, and they work to educate the public as to why these initiatives are important. States often use ESA funding to work with private landowners, providing them with the knowledge and tools that they need to protect the plants and animals living on their property. The passage of the ESA was a huge step in the right direction for

**nonprofit:** a charitable organization that uses its money to help others, rather than to make financial gain, or to make "profit"

**rambunctious:** rowdy, unruly; difficult to control

**vegan:** a person who does not consume or use any products that come from animals

# CHAPTER 3

# Volunteering and Organizations

## GETTING INVOLVED—VOLUNTEERING

If you're ready to start working with animals, volunteering is a great way to learn more about the different careers in this field. There are many different volunteer opportunities available when it comes to working with animals. No matter what volunteer path you choose, you'll finish the day knowing that you made a difference in the life of an animal that needed your help.

If you're ready to volunteer, it's a good idea to start by figuring out how often you'd like to volunteer, the type of organization for which you'd like to work, and how long you'd like your volunteer commitment to last. Many animal organizations will welcome any help that you are able give,

*When working as a volunteer there are times when you will be expected to do some dirty work such as cleaning out the kennels.*

even if that means only volunteering for a few hours a month, or only having a short time period in which you are able to volunteer. As a volunteer, you'll be expected to do some of the dirty work, like cleaning and grooming, and play with the animals, giving them love, attention, and entertainment. Working as a volunteer is a great stepping-stone to starting a career working with animals.

Organizations will often interview volunteers prior to accepting their help. While these positions are unpaid, organizations still depend on volunteers every day to keep things running smoothly, so they need to make sure they are working with people who are dependable and responsible. Some organizations will

also require a background check prior to the interview to ensure that the volunteers they hire are law-abiding citizens without a criminal record.

If you're asked to interview for a volunteer position, treat it the same way that you would treat an interview for a paid job: dress professionally, bring a copy of your résumé, and research the organization beforehand so that you can ask your interviewer pertinent questions. If you're volunteering to fulfill a school requirement (such as community service hours for a graduation project), find out ahead of time how many hours you need to volunteer and whether all of those hours need to be

*Volunteers are sometimes expected to help train dogs for rehoming. This dog is being trained to sit on command.*

completed within a certain time frame. Be sure to present this information to your interviewer to make sure they are able to accommodate your needs.

When you decide to accept a position as a volunteer, you and your new supervisor will go over a schedule of your volunteer hours. You won't be working on your own right away. It's likely that a seasoned volunteer will walk you through the day-to-day tasks of

*There are many voluntary roles to choose from at rescue centers. This girl has volunteered to groom one of the horses, an important task that needs performing daily.*

## MY FIRST WEEKS OF VOLUNTEERING

During my gap year, I volunteered at an animal shelter that provided homes for unwanted and abandoned animals. When I first started working there, I was asked to spend my first few weeks working alongside a more experienced volunteer who had been working at the shelter for some time. Our first job of the morning was to check that all the animals had a comfortable night. Next, we fed and watered them. Next, we cleaned out all the cages and runs throughly. My favorite part of the morning followed. It was our job to exercise and help to train the dogs at the center. This was great fun and very rewarding. It was lovely to see how the dogs flourished and how their confidence grew over time. After all the fun, we spent the afternoon working in the office doing paperwork and after that prepared all the animals for the night. —Dan Jones.

the organization. They're there to help you—it's ok if you need to ask questions along the way. Just like with a regular job, it's important that you show up on time and work for your full shift. It's important to let your supervisor know if you are unable to work a scheduled shift as early as possible. Your co-volunteers, supervisor, and the animals are counting on you to do the work you agreed to do.

As you gain experience as a volunteer, you may eventually receive a promotion! Some volunteers gain greater responsibility in working with customers, while others might become in charge of managing volunteers. If you're interested in more responsibility in your volunteer position, talk to your supervisor about the possibility of stepping into a leadership role.

## ANIMAL SHELTERS

As an animal shelter volunteer, you may have a wide range of responsibilities. You will likely help with feeding and watering, grooming, and entertainment. Many shelters have a cat room in which you can simply play with them, helping them to get exercise. You will probably be asked to take a dog-walking class before exercising the dogs at the shelter, and this is necessary for a few reasons. First, some dogs can be **rambunctious**, and it's important that all volunteers train the dogs to walk well on the leash in the same way. Otherwise, the dogs could get confused and struggle to make progress.

It's also key that you are taught how to control the dog you are walking to keep them safe from fellow pedestrians—and fellow pedestrians safe from the dog! When you walk dogs at the shelter, the dog

*Animal shelters are always looking for dog walkers. This is an ideal voluntary job for people who have time on their hands and enjoy some good exercise.*

may be given a vest to wear that says, "Adopt me!" You'll be trained on how to interact with anyone who stops you on your walk and would like more information about adopting the dog.

As a volunteer, you may also be responsible for working at the front desk. This could mean that you'll be in charge of answering phones, helping potential adopters fill out their paperwork, and assisting pet owners who come in seeking medical care. You'll also be expected to roll up your sleeves and pitch in with cleaning litter boxes and dog crates, which can include sweeping, mopping, and doing laundry. While these aren't the most glamorous parts of the volunteer experience, they are vital to help the animals stay clean and healthy.

While volunteering at an shelter can be incredibly rewarding, it can also be emotionally difficult. Some animal shelters have policies that require that they euthanize pets that have not been adopted within a certain timeframe. This can make you very sad if you have developed a connection—it's easy to become attached to an animal you've been working with. Sometimes there just isn't enough money available to keep the animals indefinitely. It's important to remember that by volunteering at the shelter, you are helping the shelter dedicate more of its resources to helping and finding homes for animals in need. If you do not feel that you would be able to handle this type of experience but you are still interested in volunteering at an animal shelter, you may want to see if there are no-kill shelters in your area.

*When walking a dog for a shelter either you or the dog may wear an item of clothing to advertise that the dog needs to be rehomed.*

*Rescue animals may have suffered from abuse and neglect and in some cases can be hard to handle. However, with kindness and gentle handling, nearly all of them will learn to trust again.*

## RESCUE ORGANIZATIONS

Volunteering at a rescue organization is another option. These associations typically work with one specific type of animal—only dogs, only cats, or only horses, for example. If you're interested in eventually pursuing a career in a specific type of veterinary medicine, it may make sense for you to volunteer with a species-specific rescue. Some organizations are even breed specific—for example, there are rescues that only accept beagles.

As a rescue volunteer, many of your responsibilities will be the same as those of a shelter volunteer. You'll provide animals with food and water, give them basic grooming, and make sure they are getting enough exercise. After some time and training, you may also assist your supervisor with picking up animals that have been relinquished to the rescue. This can be hard on everyone involved, especially when the owner loves their pet but recognizes that they are no longer able to provide proper care.

*Animal therapy is an alternative type of treatment when animals such as dogs are used to aid a patient's recovery. Each dog has to pass a specific test and be trained to ensure that it is suitable for the work.*

Many animals that are rescued are in very bad shape. They can be infected with parasites, starving, or suffering from disease, or they may have been abused. While it may be difficult to see animals in these or other heartbreaking states, it's important to remember that you are there to help them. By volunteering at a rescue organization, you are providing an animal with love and hope.

## ANIMAL THERAPY

If you have a dog and are interested in helping others, animal therapy may be a good volunteer option for you. You and your dog will go through a series of training classes. Your pet will be taught how to be gentle with the people who your dog visits, and you'll be taught specific commands to keep your dog on track. At the end of the training classes, which usually last a couple of months, you and your dog need to pass a therapy dog test. This will involve your instructor watching you instruct your dog to follow several commands, as well as making sure your dog can easily socialize with other people and other animals.

*Therapy dogs are not just confined to hospital visits. They also have a role at senior care homes. Research shows that interaction with therapy dogs can improve the well-being of many residents.*

After this test is passed and you have proof that your dog has been examined by a vet, has been given a clean bill of health, and has all of their required vaccinations, you and your dog will be able to provide therapy to people in hospitals, including children, and nursing homes. It's important to talk to the hospital or nursing home you would like to visit to set up an appointment when you will arrive. Often, patients and residents are very excited to be able to play with a dog, and the event is advertised to them ahead of time.

Many patients report that they have lower levels of stress after a session with a therapy dog. Your dog won't be asked to do any tricks—they'll simply relax while patients shower them with love and attention. The benefits of pet therapy go both ways. Your dog will enjoy the attention and helping others, and the patients will have a boost in mood from getting to spend some time with a dog.

While your dog will be the star of the show, many patients will want to talk to you as well, usually to share stories of the dogs they have or had in the past. Providing a listening ear means the world to many of them.

Training your dog to become a therapy dog is a great way for you to bond with your pet, as well as provide a valuable service to your community.

## SERVICE DOG TRAINING

Many people with disabilities depend on service dogs to help them complete their daily activities, such as going to the grocery store, doing laundry, and even going for a walk. Service dogs undergo intensive training before they are matched with an owner. There are many organizations that train dogs that will eventually become service dogs, and these organizations often accept volunteers.

There are three different types of service dogs—guide dogs, hearing dogs, and service dogs—and therapy dogs.

Guide dogs provide assistance to people who are visually impaired, helping their owners navigate the environment around them. Guide dogs are trained to help people walk on busy sidewalks, go up and down the stairs, and even cross the road. These dogs can complete a number of activities for their owner in their home as well, such as turning the lights on and off, opening doors, and alerting them to people who are outside the house.

Hearing dogs help to alert hearing impaired people to important sounds, such as an ambulance siren or a doorbell

*There are organizations that train service dogs to help people with disabilities perform daily tasks. You can get involved by volunteering to help with a service dog's training.*

*Service dogs, such as those who assist the blind, are usually trained from the time they were puppies and require special and rigorous training. However, some organizations use volunteers to train rescue dogs to assist people with other disabilities such as wheelchair users.*

ringing. Both people who are deaf and people with partial hearing loss benefit greatly from this kind of assistance.

Service dogs help people with other needs, such as people with autism or those who require a wheelchair. The most common types of service dogs are golden retrievers or Labrador retrievers. Some service dogs assist owners who have epilepsy, as the dogs are able to detect when their owner is about to have a seizure. Then the dog can signal the owner, or others nearby, so they know the person is going to need assistance very shortly. A person with epilepsy can lie down safely before the seizure starts instead of falling down unexpectedly and potentially hurting themselves.

Therapy dogs are very different from service dogs. While a service dog is trained to assist one particular owner only, therapy dogs travel and help many people. In order for an animal to be trained as a therapy dog, only a few months of intense classes are required. In contrast, service dog training can take up to two years and is often followed by even more training to teach the dog the specific needs of their owner.

*Assistance Dogs International welcomes volunteers to its organization. This can ultimately lead to a job as a qualified trainer. This young collie is in training to become an autism assistance dog.*

A working therapy dog welcomes attention—it is no problem for people in the public to walk up to them and pet them—but service dogs are different. Because they are extremely focused on the needs of their owner, these dogs often wear a vest asking people to refrain from petting them or giving them attention that might distract them from their job.

## ASSISTANCE DOGS INTERNATIONAL (ADI)

As one of the most well-known service dog training organizations, if you're interested in working with or training service dogs one day, ADI stresses that it is extremely important to start as a volunteer. After volunteering, you may be able to gain employment as an apprentice. Being an apprentice means that you work with and learn from a skilled, experienced dog trainer so that you can begin to learn the trade. In time, an apprenticeship could turn into a job as a full-time service dog trainer.

# ORGANIZATIONS

If you're not able to volunteer in person right now, there are still a number of organizations that will help you learn more about working with animals. The more knowledge you have, the easier it will be to decide if a career in helping animals is right for you. With the information you learn, you'll also be able to educate others about animal welfare.

One of the most important things that humans can do for animals is simply to make other people aware of what they can do to help. You can do this through conversations, presentations in science class, or by inviting others to learn more by checking out animal welfare organizations for themselves. You can also help by raising money and donating to these organizations. Your gift will go toward helping animals in need.

## WORLD WILDLIFE FUND (WWF)

The WWF has been working for the past fifty years to protect nature and reduce threats to all species on Earth. While the WWF generally is known for protecting land and plants, a large part of their efforts are focused on protecting wildlife.

One of the unique and most well-known programs created by the WWF is the Symbolic Species Adoption program. This arrangement allows people to "adopt" an animal of their choosing, such as an African elephant, a panda, a narwhal, etc. The fee that they pay to adopt the animal goes toward the WWF's overall mission. The donor receives a stuffed toy of the animal they

*The orangutan is one of the iconic species that is part of the World Wildlife Fund's adoption program.*

**ENDANGERED SPECIES**

chose, an adoption certificate, and an information card that tells them about their animal. These symbolic adoptions are popular as birthday gifts for young children who are interested in protecting animals.

## PEOPLE FOR THE ETHICAL TREATMENT OF ANIMALS (PETA)

PETA is an organization that stands up for the rights of animals. They are known for strongly opposing the fur trade and factory farming, and for encouraging people to adopt a **vegan** lifestyle. While PETA is sometimes

*London Fashion Week in England. PETA demonstrators in cat outfits celebrate a "No Fur" fashion week.*

seen as a polarizing organization due to their strong recommendation of a vegan lifestyle, they work hard to fight for the rights of animals. PETA readily accepts volunteers, who can help fight for animal rights in a variety of ways.

If you're interested in volunteering with PETA, your volunteer supervisor will give you some different options. You may be able to man an information table at a concert or festival. You may do office work, such as filing papers, stuffing envelopes, or making phone calls. You may take part in demonstrations to raise awareness for animal rights. PETA volunteers also sometimes provide foster homes to animals in need for a few days until a more permanent placement is found. If you're passionate about animal rights, becoming a PETA volunteer might be the right move for you.

*Dating from 1866 when it was first established, ASPCA is a nonprofit organization based in New York City.*

## AMERICAN SOCIETY FOR THE PREVENTION OF CRUELTY TO ANIMALS (ASPCA)

The ASPCA is committed to protecting animals and helping animals in need. In 2017 alone, the organization rescued or helped over 47,000 animals. The ASPCA also provides free or low-cost neutering and spaying to pet owners with a financial need, therefore reducing the number of unwanted animal pregnancies. The ASPCA advocates for animal rights while placing a strong emphasis on the importance of animal adoption. Many pet owners and animal care facilities look to the ASPCA's guidelines as the gold standard on how animals should be treated.

# WHAT'S AN INTERNSHIP?

As you explore volunteer options, you may come across opportunities for internships. Internships are short-term jobs with a business or organization to help students get a glimpse into the career field while gaining valuable experience. Some internships are paid; some are unpaid. Many internships are available only to college students, but some are available to high school students. If you see an internship opportunity that interests you, call the organization and see if they would consider someone of your age and education level. If the internship is paid, it may not count toward requirements for a graduation project. If this is important to you, be sure to talk to your advisor before you accept the position.

# VOLUNTEERING AT AN ANIMAL SHELTER

*A day in the life of staff and volunteers at an*
*Animal Humane Society shelter*

# TEXT-DEPENDENT QUESTIONS

1. What is one difference between service dogs and therapy dogs?

2. What does the acronym ASPCA stand for?

3. Why would an organization request a background check for volunteers?

# RESEARCH PROJECT

Research an animal outreach organization not mentioned in this chapter. Find out when they were established, how many animals they help each year, and where their headquarters are located.

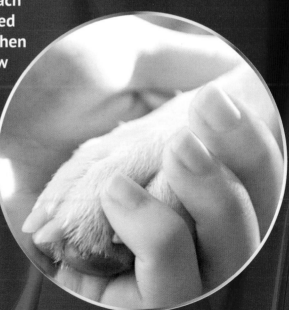

# Milestone Moment

## THE AMERICANS WITH DISABILITIES ACT

Passed in 1990, the Americans with Disabilities Act (ADA) is the main law in the United States that protects service dogs and the people with disabilities who depend on them. By law, service dogs must be specifically trained to work with only one person, meaning that this law does not apply to general therapy dogs. The service dog must be trained to do specific tasks, such as helping a blind person across the street or alerting an owner with epilepsy that a seizure is on the horizon.

Prior to the passage of the ADA, some establishments, such as restaurants, would not allow service dogs to come in, meaning that the people who depended on service dogs to help them with activities of daily living were unable to patronize these businesses. The passing of the ADA protects people with disabilities and ensures their right to use a service animal in public facilities.

The only rules for having a service animal in public—beyond the service animal being trained to work with one person and performing tasks for that person—are that the animal must be housebroken and well-behaved. While it seems like these two points are obvious, they are important to note due to the fact that some people unfortunately attempt to pass off their untrained pets as service dogs. It's also required that a recognized service dog school has trained the service dog.

## WORDS TO UNDERSTAND

**activities of daily living:** these include walking down the street, opening doors, turning lights off and on, and using public transportation—all things that may present challenges to differently abled people

**bachelor's degree:** a status category that is awarded after a four-year course of study at a college or university

**graduate degree:** a status category that is awarded after completing a master's, doctorate, or PhD program; typically must be preceded by gaining a bachelor's degree

**living spaces:** for animals, the places where they live might be cages or crates, tanks, outdoor runs, barns or sheds, or specific rooms in a building dedicated to a certain kind of animal; whatever the type, living spaces need to be kept clean and adjusted to other environmental conditions specific to the occupant

# CHAPTER 4

## Education, Training, and Qualifications

### EDUCATION

People of all education levels are able to work with animals. From high school graduates to those with advanced degrees, there are places for all in the world of animal welfare work.

*If it is your dream to work with animals, a career at a zoo may be the right choice. Ultimately though, your qualifications will dictate the number of opportunities available to you.*

## PRE-HIGH SCHOOL GRADUATE

Even if you are still in high school, it's possible to become employed and gain experience in working with animals. Many animal welfare organizations are happy to take on high school students who are interested in learning more about animals as part-time employees. You may be required to take certain training before working with animals. It's often easier to be hired for this type of employment if you first work as a volunteer. If you are already volunteering and are interested in transitioning to paid work, talk with your volunteer supervisor to learn more about available opportunities.

## HIGH SCHOOL GRADUATE LEVEL

People with high school diplomas are able to work in animal shelters, veterinary offices, zoos, and rescue centers, but they are not permitted to carry out medical procedures. Typically, people with high school diplomas work in direct animal care. This can include grooming, feeding, maintenance of **living spaces**, and exercising/entertaining animals. Over time, it is possible for someone with a high school diploma to receive on-the-job training and be promoted to a position typically reserved for someone with a higher level of education. Some facilities also consider volunteer experience as education, and this can help someone with a high school diploma receive a promotion to a higher level as well.

## BACHELOR'S DEGREE LEVEL

With a four-year **bachelor's degree** from an accredited university, opportunities begin to open up to do more advanced work with animals. Animal nurses and professional dog trainers usually require a four-year degree. Many people who have their bachelor's degree and want to continue their education become employed at this level while pursuing a higher-education degree.

Some people with bachelor's degrees are involved in the direct care of animals, but many are involved in operational/managerial positions within animal welfare organizations. These positions may include: supervising volunteers; supervising building activities; managing the front desk of a shelter, rescue organization, or vet's office; or assisting top-level professionals with their daily tasks, such as scheduling medical procedures.

All zoologists have bachelor's degrees, and a person can often obtain a position doing research for conservation organizations at this level. Some organizations will even pay for

*There are some careers that are available only to people who have a bachelor's degree. An animal nurse or police dog trainer are both roles that usually require applicants to have completed their degree.*

# A ZOOKEEPER ON CALL

Usually a zookeeper's job is typically nine-to-five. However, staff at a zoo will invariably be asked to share staying on call with their colleagues so that everyone gets a turn to take time out. Just like people who look after human beings, there might be emergencies that a zookeeper needs to take care of. As a zookeeper you might be asked to take care of a sick animal at night or watch out for an animal that is about to give birth. In fact, there are many occasions where animals need a zookeeper's care outside of the normal working day. If you are thinking of working in a zoo, the likelihood of out-of-hours work is something that should be considered before you apply for the job.

their zoologists to obtain advanced **graduate degrees**. While zoologists can certainly make a living at this level, most prefer to go on to higher education so that they can conduct their own research studies and start their own projects within conservation organizations.

## GRADUATE-DEGREE LEVEL

Most graduate-level programs in animal care (including the course of study required to become a veterinarian) involve four additional years of study after earning a bachelor's degree. The first three years of graduate school are spent learning theoretical concepts of veterinary medicine, such as animal biology and physiology, animal nutrition, and animal behavior. This means lots of studying, virtual surgeries, basic animal care, and observation of practicing veterinarians. The final year of graduate school is spent completing high-level procedures under the supervision of an experienced, licensed veterinarian.

After graduating from veterinary school, all graduates must take a licensing exam in order to legally practice animal medicine. Some accredited schools even allow up-and-coming veterinarians to take this test up to eight months before graduation. In the time between graduating from veterinary school and passing the licensing test, many vets work as techs in veterinary offices, studying for the licensing exam in their spare time.

After earning a doctor of veterinary medicine degree, some vets choose to continue their education in order to become an expert on a particular type of animal, or in a particular field of medicine (such as emergency medicine).

Many zoologists, animal biologists, and animal behaviorists receive education at the graduate-school level. While getting their graduate degree, it's normal for people in animal studies to conduct research and write research papers, informing others in the field of their findings. Working at this level is ideal for people who are interested in becoming pioneers in animal studies.

*Veterinarians are very highly trained. Once qualified, some choose to continue their education in order to specialize further.*

# TRAINING

Some career paths, such as working in a shelter or as a vet tech, offer on-the-job training. There are also technical and trade schools that will help high school students and graduates learn about animal care without requiring a college education. In these types of career fields, it's likely that workers will receive promotions and salary increases as they spend more time on the job. Sometimes the employer is even willing to pay for additional schooling or training if the employee signs a contract stating that they will remain employed with that business or office for a specified period of time.

While some training takes place on the job, other types of training require official schooling, such as attending school to learn how to become a guide dog trainer or learning how to groom animals professionally. Typically, these types of jobs require licensure that is granted after a certain amount of schooling and the passing of certain tests.

Since new advancements in animal medicine are made constantly, it's important for people in the animal welfare field to constantly learn more about the animals they work with by continuing their education. This does not necessarily mean that another degree is required. Learning from others in the field, taking classes, and observing other offices can all give animal welfare professionals new ideas on how to be the best they can be at their job.

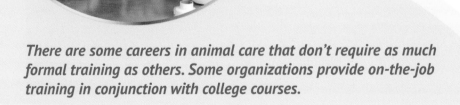

*There are some careers in animal care that don't require as much formal training as others. Some organizations provide on-the-job training in conjunction with college courses.*

*Training to be a veterinarian takes long hours and a good deal of dedication. Veterinarians must have a passion for animal care and be prepared for the academic challenges to get qualified.*

## QUALIFICATIONS

While all jobs in the animal welfare field require some type of education ranging from high school to advanced degrees, many jobs have certain qualifications as well, such as a certain number of years of experience working with animals. Organizations often accept volunteer hours in order to fulfill these requirements. This is one of the reasons why it is so important to have a good recommendation from your volunteer supervisor, even if you never end up working for the organization as a paid employee.

As the education level for particular jobs increases, the qualifications tend to increase as well. At the bachelor's level, many jobs will require you to have years of experience at the post–high school level. At the graduate level, many jobs will require you to have years of experience at the post-bachelor's level. It's a good idea to constantly look for new ways to gain experience working with animals so that you are able to continually advance in the field.

## DO ANIMAL WELFARE WORKERS EVER ADOPT THE ANIMALS THEY WORK WITH?

The short answer: Yes! Every so often, an animal comes into an office or organization, and one of the workers forms a special bond with that animal. Most animal care workers have a few pets that they felt close to and chose to adopt. It's important to remember that while you may want to take all of the animals in need home with you, there are only so many to which you can provide adequate attention and care. Some veterinary offices and shelters even adopt "office pets" that socialize with customers during office hours and sleep in the office after closing time.

## BECOMING A VETERINARY ASSISTANT

*Learn more about what it takes to become a veterinary assistant*

Kristy Sutton
Veterinary Assistant

# TEXT-DEPENDENT QUESTIONS

1. What is a job in animal welfare that could be obtained with a bachelor's degree?

2. Name one animal welfare job that requires a graduate degree.

3. Can high school students get paid to work with animals?

# RESEARCH PROJECT

Choose one of the graduate- or bachelor-level careers from this chapter, and research a program at a university near you that would allow you to go into one of these fields. How many years of schooling and experience would you need to be considered for employment in your chosen position?

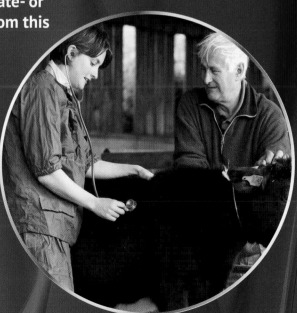

# Milestone Moment

## DOG FIGHTING BECOMES A FELONY

While the Animal Welfare Act of 1996 contains specific laws that prohibit dog fighting, engaging in this horrific behavior did not become a felony until 1990. While the specific laws and penalties differ in each state, the act of dog fighting is a felony across the nation. This was a major victory for animals and animal welfare advocates, but there is still much work to be done. Dog fighting is kept highly secret, and in most areas, law enforcement and animal welfare officials have a very difficult time infiltrating dog-fighting rings.

Dog fighting is brutal. By employing abuse, isolation, and sometimes illegal drugs, some people train animals to be highly aggressive. When dogs lose fights, they are sometimes executed in a public manner, as a part of the "entertainment" of the fight and as punishment for embarrassing their owner. In the past, this terrible form of animal abuse was sometimes punished by giving the offender only a small fine or a relatively inconsequential mark on their record. Now that dog fighting is a felony in all states, being convicted of the crime carries a mandatory sentence of at least one year in prison.

In 2014, the Animal Fighting Spectator Prohibition Act was signed into law, making it a crime to watch dog fighting. Additional fines are imposed on anyone who brings a child under the age of sixteen to watch dog fighting. While there is still a long way to go in putting an end to animal fighting, making dog fighting a felony is a huge step in

**felony:** a violent crime that is more serious than a misdemeanor, is punishable by jail time, or, in extreme cases, death

**paraprofessional:** a person who performs some aspects of a professional's job, such as the person in the office who is responsible for cleaning the vet's medical tools

**prohibit:** prevent by authority

# CHAPTER 5

## Salaries, Job Outlook, and Work Satisfaction

### SALARIES

Just like there is a wide variety of jobs within the animal care career path, there is a tremendous variety of salaries as well. Some animal care workers, like shelter employees, may be paid hourly. Others, such as veterinarians or shelter supervisors, typically receive a yearly salary. Some jobs in this field include vacation days and benefits (such as health and dental insurance), while others do not. Sometimes animal care work payment is calculated on a case-by-case basis. For example, a professional dog trainer may decide on a fee per training lesson, or a groomer may decide on a charge based on the size of the pet and its type of fur.

# WHAT'S BURNOUT?

Burnout is when someone becomes physically or mentally unable to do their job well due to excessive work-related stress. Some fields of animal welfare work are prone to burnout, including rescue work and animal shelter work. While people in these positions tend to care deeply for animals, this can actually hurt their work satisfaction. It is hard to deal with the reality of shelters and rescues. Frequently they do not have all the resources that they need to help all of the animals that they would like to help. It can also be mentally and emotionally taxing to deal with pet owners who have not taken good care of their pets or to have to remove an animal from a home in which they are loved but not well-cared-for.

Burnout affects people in all career fields to some degree, but it is especially common in the helping/caring professions. Burnout can be prevented by arriving at and leaving work on time (instead of showing up early and leaving late), not discussing work too much at home, and taking regular vacations and time off to give yourself a mental break. Burnout can also affect volunteers. If you're a volunteer and you feel that you're beginning to experience burnout, it's important to talk to your supervisor to come up with a plan so that you can keep volunteering effectively.

Salary also varies based on experience and education. It's important to remember that while a salary for a certain job may seem very high, these top-level positions require a lot of education. It takes time and money to acquire the schooling needed to work up to a high salary level.

## ANIMAL SHELTER CAREERS

As mentioned above, most animal shelter workers are paid on an hourly basis, with the pay rate determined by how long they've worked at the shelter, how much experience they have working with animals, and their job performance. Shelter managers are typically paid by salary, with an average of $35,000 per year. Executive directors of animal shelters (the people responsible for supervising the managers) make an average of $59,000 per year. Veterinarians are typically the highest-paid professionals in animal shelters, with an average salary of $75,000 per year.

## RESCUE CENTER CAREERS

Many rescue centers rely heavily on volunteers, with only a few paid employees running the show behind the scenes. An executive director of a rescue center typically makes a little bit less than an executive director of an animal shelter, at approximately $50,000 per year. A director of operations at a rescue center typically makes around $41,000 per year. This person is in charge of the logistics of the rescue center, including keeping track of necessary supplies and selecting contractors to perform building maintenance. Directors of operations also sometimes act as a human resources department within an organization, ensuring that all employees and volunteers complete necessary paperwork and get paid on time.

*Pay rates within the animal care sector vary greatly. Generally, the higher qualified the individual is, the higher the pay.*

Animal charity workers frequently work for and with rescue organizations to help them raise funds for their cause. On average, fundraisers for animal charities make around $49,000 per year. These numbers are only averages because rescues vary greatly in the amount of funding they have available. Therefore, the salaries of their employees can vary greatly as well.

## VETERINARY OFFICES

Within a veterinary office, there are many different jobs that need to be done. Maintenance workers and janitors are needed for the safe, sanitary operation of the office as a business, and groundskeepers make sure the property is clean and attractive for the customers and visiting dogs. These positions are typically paid on an hourly basis that depends on the person's experience level, job performance, and how long they have worked at the veterinary office.

*A front desk worker's duties will include a variety of tasks, including responding to customer inquiries, scheduling appointments, answering phones, and other hands-on duties.*

Paraprofessionals, such as veterinary technicians, typically make around $32,000 per year. Some veterinary technicians are paid hourly, while others are paid on a yearly salary. A veterinary technician's pay may also be dependent on their personal job description, which might include a variety of tasks, including working the front desk, scheduling appointments and answering phones, cleaning up after animals, feeding and grooming, and assisting with medical procedures. In some offices, clerical staff and an office manager take care of the front reception area, and the vet techs take care of animal-related tasks.

*Veterinary technicians have a number of roles including assisting with some medical procedures.*

Animal nurses earn an average salary of $51,000 per year, with the potential to make more if they're willing to take on overtime shifts or shifts outside of their typical work schedule.

Veterinarians make the most money at a veterinary office, with a typical salary of approximately $97,000 for vets who take care of small animals only, and $103,000 for vets who work with large animals, like cows and horses. Many veterinarians actually own their offices, which has many benefits. They are able to choose their operating hours, make their own schedules, and, of course, keep the profits that the office earns. But a single vet will get called on nights and weekends for emergencies, so some office veterinarians will share a practice and the office so they can see more animals, earn more money, and be able to take scheduled time off.

All of these professions—vet techs, animal nurses, and vets—can also work in emergency animal medicine, either in an office building or, in larger cities, a veterinary hospital. This type of work typically pays more than

*A zoologist has an interesting profession that in some instances involves traveling all over the world. This zoologist is working at a rhinoceros sanctuary in Kenya.*

working in a typical office due to the unusual hours involved. Some emergency medicine vets even make house calls to take care of or euthanize sick or injured animals. While the pay is higher, the stress level is also higher due to the long hours and often emotional situations that emergency vets face.

Some veterinarians work at an office practice with normal hours most of the time and then also work one weekend per month at an emergency veterinary medicine clinic or hospital. This allows them to participate in high-stress, lifesaving medical care for pets while also running an office and providing more routine care the rest of the time.

## ZOOLOGIST

A zoologist, also known as a wildlife biologist, typically makes approximately $50,000 per year. The pay can vary widely depending on whom the zoologist works for. A lead zoologist at a top national zoo is

*The number of jobs in animal welfare and care has grown massively due to an increase in pet ownership. People who work with animals usually find that their career is both rewarding and worthwhile.*

likely to make more than a zoologist working in a small research lab during graduate school.

One of the unique advantages to being a zoologist is the opportunity to travel. Many zoologists travel to other countries and continents to study wildlife that we do not have in the United States. While they might not make as much money as some other positions in the animal welfare world, they will almost certainly have incredible experiences and unique memories that they would not find while working in an office.

## JOB OUTLOOK

Most career paths that involve animal welfare have shown steady growth recently, and it's likely that this trend will continue as pet owners demand more services for their pets. Many young adults are waiting until later in life to have children, and so they spend the money that would typically go toward childcare on their "fur babies." This has resulted in a booming pet services industry. In 2014, over $58 billion was spent in the pet services industry.

Sadly, this has also resulted in more animals in shelters, as some people who adopt or purchase pets are not fully aware of the responsibility that is involved. The need for animal shelter workers and animal rescue workers continues to grow with time.

## WORK SATISFACTION

The reasons that people want to work with animals are myriad. There is a deep sense of satisfaction that comes from helping those that cannot help themselves. There is no feeling in the world that compares to saving an animal. Many animal welfare workers report a deep sense of satisfaction in the work that they do, even when they have to deal with parts of the job that are emotionally difficult, such as comforting owners after the euthanasia of a beloved pet.

The level of satisfaction that a person experiences with their job in the world of animal welfare can depend on a few different things. A person who is a dog trainer, training service dogs to help people who are disabled, may have a very different experience in their workday than an emergency veterinarian. A person's attitude, the area in which their job is located, and

*Job satisfaction is high in most caring professions. Those helping animals in need want to make a real difference to an animal's well-being.*

their relationship with their coworkers and/or their supervisor can all contribute to how they feel about their job.

It's important to consider how much daily contact with animals you would like if you're looking for a career in this field. If you want to spend all day, every day, taking care of furry friends, you probably wouldn't have a high level of job satisfaction as an animal charity fundraiser. Becoming a dog groomer or dog trainer might make more sense for your interests. If you're interested in the medical side of animal welfare, you'll probably want to work in a veterinarian's office, specifically in direct animal care.

If you're not sure which path you'd like to take, it's a great idea to volunteer or complete an internship in a few different areas. This can give you a sense of which type of work would make you feel most satisfied before you dive into fulfilling the educational requirements for a career.

*Marine biologists study life in the sea. In this case, marine biologist are releasing a seal back into the sea.*

## A DAY IN THE LIFE OF A NATIONAL PARK RANGER

National park rangers play an important in animal conservation. The are also responsible for keeping animals safe and ensuring that visitors to national parks follow the rules and regulations.

Park rangers report very high levels of job satisfaction, but many say that it's important to be ok with spending lots of time by yourself. If you're the type of person who needs regular conversation with coworkers to stay happy throughout the day, becoming a park ranger may not be a good choice for you.

## A CAREER IN ZOOLOGY

*Learn more about if a career as a zoologist might be a good fit for you*

or remote mountainous and woodland regions that may have few modern comforts.

1. What is a job in animal welfare that could be obtained with a bachelor's degree?

2. Name one animal welfare job that requires a graduate degree.

3. Can high school students get paid to work with animals?

## RESEARCH PROJECT

Interview someone in an animal welfare career on their job satisfaction. (Remember, it is not ok to ask anyone how much they make.) Compare their answers to the information in this chapter and explain whether the person you interviewed seems more or less satisfied with their career than the average animal welfare worker.

# SERIES GLOSSARY OF KEY TERMS

| | |
|---|---|
| **abuse:** | Wrong or unfair treatment or use. |
| **academic:** | Of or relating to schools and education. |
| **advancement:** | Progression to a higher stage of development. |
| **anxiety:** | Fear or nervousness about what might happen. |
| **apprentice:** | A person who learns a job or skill by working for a fixed period of time for someone who is very good at that job or skill. |
| **culture:** | A way of thinking, behaving, or working that exists in a place or organization (such as a business.) |
| **donation:** | The making of an especially charitable gift. |
| **empathy:** | The ability to understand and share the feelings of others. |
| **endangered species:** | A specific type of plant or animal that is likely to become extinct in the near future. |
| **ethics:** | The study of morality, or right and wrong. |
| **food security:** | Having reliable access to a steady source of nutritious food. |
| **intern:** | A student or recent graduate in a special field of study (as medicine or teaching) who works for a period of time to gain practical experience. |
| **mediation:** | Intervention between conflicting parties to promote reconciliation, settlement, or compromise. |
| **nonprofit:** | A charitable organization that uses its money to help others, rather than to make financial gain, aka "profit." |
| **ombudsman:** | A person who advocates for the needs and wants of an individual in a facility anonymously so that the individual receiving care can voice complaints without fear of consequences. |
| **pediatrician:** | A doctor who specializes in the care of babies and children. |
| **perpetrator:** | A person who commits a harmful or illegal act. |
| **poverty:** | The state of one who lacks a usual or socially acceptable amount of money or material possessions. |
| **retaliate:** | To do something bad to someone who has hurt you or treated you badly; to get revenge against someone. |
| **salary:** | The amount of money you receive each year for the work you perform. |
| **sanctuary:** | A place of refuge and protection. |
| **stress:** | Something that causes strong feelings of worry or anxiety. |
| **substance abuse:** | Excessive use of a drug (such as alcohol, narcotics, or cocaine); use of a drug without medical justification. |
| **syndrome:** | A group of signs and symptoms that occur together and characterize a particular abnormality or condition. |
| **therapist:** | A person trained in methods of treatment and rehabilitation other than the use of drugs or surgery. |

# ORGANIZATIONS TO CONTACT

**Adopt-a-Pet.com:** 310 N. Indian Hill Blvd., #800, Claremont, CA 91711. Phone: 1-800-Save-A-Pet 1-800-728-3273. E-mail: info@adoptapet.com Website: www.adoptapet.com

**Animal Welfare Institute:** 900 Pennsylvania Ave., Washington, DC 20003. Phone: (202) 337-2332. E-mail: awi@awionline.org Website: www.awionline.org

**The Anti-Cruelty Society:** 157 West Grand Ave., Chicago, IL 60654. Phone: (312) 644-8338 Fax: (312) 644-3878. E-mail: info@anticruelty.org Website: www.anticruelty.org

**Best Friends Animal Society:** 5001 Angel Canyon Rd., Kanab, Utah 84741-5000. Phone: 435-644-2001. E-mail: info@bestfriends.org Website: www.bestfriends.org

**International Fund for Animal Welfare:** 1400 16th St. NW, Suite 510, Washington, DC 20036. Phone: (202) 536-1900. E-mail: info@ifaw.org Website: www.ifaw.org

**RedRover:** PO Box 188890 Sacramento, CA 95818 Phone: (916) 429-2457. E-mail info@redrover.org Website: https://redrover.org/

**SAVE the WHALES:** 1192 Waring St., Seaside, CA 93955. Phone: (831)-899-9957. E-mail: maris@savethewhales.org Website: www.savethewhales.org

**Thoroughbred Charities of America (TCA):** PO Box 910668, Lexington, KY 40591. Phone: (831)-899-9957. E-mail: info@tca.org Website: www.tca.org

# INTERNET RESOURCES

**www.aspca.org**

The American Society for the Prevention of Cruelty to Animals promotes the fact that animals are entitled to respect and care and asserts that the ethical treatment of animals needs to be protected by law. Visit their site to learn about taking action to encourage lawmakers to support animal rights, how to adopt a pet, and how you can help animals in your area.

**www.equinerescuenetwork.com**

The Equine Rescue Network harnesses the power of social media to find homes for horses that are at risk of neglect or death. By simply sharing their posts about horses on your social media sites, you're able to make a difference for animal welfare.

**www.humanesociety.org**

Caring for over 100,000 animals each year, the Humane Society works to create a humane world for both animals and people through education, hands-on care, and creating legal change. Use this site to learn more about the atrocities that some animals face and find out what you can do to help.

**www.nature.org**

The Nature Conservancy's mission is simple—to protect nature, both for people today and for future generations. Use their site to learn more about climate change, endangered species, and what you can do today to protect nature for the generations to come.

**www.worldwildlife.org**

The World Wildlife Fund is a nonprofit organization that is dedicated to protecting animals and their environment. Use this site to learn more about endangered animals and what you can do to help them.

# FURTHER READING

Dauer, Joal and Elizabeth Ridley. *Saving Sadie: How A Dog That No One Wanted Inspired the World*. New York City: Citadel, 2017.

Efthymiadis, Ted. *Thriving Dog Trainers: An Indispensable Tool to Help You Start or Repair Your Dog Training Business*. North Charleston, SC: CreateSpace Independent Publishing Platform, 2018.

Goldberg, Marc and The Monks of New Skete. *Let Dogs Be Dogs: Understanding Canine Nature and Mastering the Art of Living with Your Dog*. New York City: Little, Brown, and Company, 2017.

Scott, Traer. *Finding Homes: Shelter Dogs and Their Stories*. New York: Princeton Architectural Press, 2015.

Zheutlin, Peter. *Rescue Road: One Man, Thirty Thousand Dogs, and a Million Miles on the Last Hope Highway*. Naperville, IL: Sourcebooks, 2015.

# INDEX

# AUTHOR'S BIOGRAPHY

AMANDA TURNER is a former biology teacher and a current animal lover. She has spent many years volunteering with various animal welfare organizations along the East Coast. Currently, Elizabeth lives in Dayton, Ohio, with her husband and son, as well as their rescue beagle-boxer mix, Stella, and their 19-pound rescue Maine coon cat, Titan.

# CREDITS

VIDEOS
Page 32 Alecia Blackhall: http://x-qr.net/1Dpb
page 50 Animal Humane Society: http://x-qr.net/1HVy
page 60 American College of Healthcare: http://x-qr.net/1DGh
page 72 YourFreeCareerTest.com: http://x-qr.net/1DcT